김혜영 시집
A Collection of Hae Young Kim's Poems

한영대역판
Korean-English Edition

바람의 언덕
Hill of Wind

휘원徽園 김 혜 영

Hye Young KIM

(Pseudonym : Graceful Knoll)

※ 평소 써온 글을 모아 육순(六旬)에 즈음하여 시집으로 발간합니다.

徽團 김혜영, 瑞婿 홍호준

필자 김혜영, 홍호준(남편), 홍승만(아들), 홍자은(딸)

김혜영 시집
A Collection of Hae Young Kim's Poems

한영대역판
Korean-English Edition

Hill of Wind

휘원徽園 김 혜 영
Hye Young KIM
(Pseudonym : Graceful Knoll)

Doosoncomm Publishing Co. Book

시집을 내면서

　나의 부모님의 고향을 지척에 두고 한 번도 가보지 못하고 한 세상 살아가면서 내 심연을 오직 종교의 힘으로 채워가며 살아왔건만 내면에 갇혀 있던 시심이 꿈틀대는 것은 삶에 저녁놀이 드리우는 이제야 느끼게 되었습니다. 그런데 조심스럽게 시를 써서 책으로 남기고 싶은 욕망이 생기게 되었습니다. 봄이 와서 꽃이 피고 여름 지나 가을 추수의 계절을 맞이하듯 모든 겸허한 마음으로 글을 모았습니다. 나의 여행 중에서 알프스의 몽블랑을 보며 무한한 감동에 탄성도 질러보았고, 몽골의 가도 가도 나무 한 포기 없는 황량한 들판에서 오묘한 대자연에 가슴 벅차오름도 느껴 보았습니다. 그래서 시詩로써 영혼의 노래를 부르려 시詩에 대한 초보로서 열심히 시詩 공부를 하고 있었습니다.

　언젠가 나의 여행에 있어서 여행기를 하나 남기려던 꿈이 이제 이루어져 아주 미약하기는 하지만 작은 나의 마음이 태어났습니다. 이것이 독자의 마음에 작은 행복의 홀씨가 되었으면 좋겠습니다. 저의 삶을 늘 푸른 초원으로 인도하여 주신 신께 감사드립니다.

　특히 지금까지 제 곁에서 말없이 든든하게 도와주신 남편과 함께 기쁨을 나눕니다. 그리고 부족한 저를 격려해주시고 시집의 탄생을 도와주신 우전 최원철 교수님께 감사드립니다.

2011년 9월

김 혜 영

Presenting the Collection of Poems

While I lived in this life unable to visit my nearby parent's hometown, I sought to fill my internal abyss with the power of religion, but now I realized that the poetic turn of mind that was trapped inside me began to wriggle in the sunset in my life. I began to have the desire to make a collection with the poems that I have written carefully. As if flowers blossom in a spring and facing the harvesting season of fall after summer, I collected my writings with a humble mind. While traveling, I exclaimed from the endless impression while looking at Mont Blanc in the Alps, and in Mongolia, I felt the overflowing impression from the profound and mysterious nature when I crossed the bleak fields where there were no trees no matter how far I went. As a beginner poet, I am studying poetry to learn to sing about the soul.

My dream to writing a journal about my trips has been realized, and although it is not perfect, my little heart is now newly born. I hope this can be a spore of little joy to you, the readers, and I thank God for always guiding me to green pastures.

Especially, I would like to share the joy with my husband, who has been silently supporting me. I would also like to thank Professor Wonchul Choi (Pseudonym : Rain-Blessed Field) who has encouraged me and helped me to complete this collection of poems.

September 2011

Hyeyoung Kim

| 목차 |

시집을 내면서 _ 6
서시 「바람의 언덕」 _ 14

노란 은행잎 _ 16
시누이 _ 18
여행 _ 20
가을 산 _ 22
바다 _ 24
부나비 _ 26
거가대교 _ 28
겨울의 길목에서 _ 32
겨울 바다 _ 34
바람의 언덕 _ 36
매미 _ 38
여름 들녘 _ 40
고향 _ 42
자작나무 숲 _ 44
정들면 내 고향 _ 46
소나기 _ 48
괌 여행 _ 50
비엔나의 밤 _ 52
에페소 여행 _ 54
회상 _ 56

| Contents |

Presenting the Collection of Poems _ 7

Prologue 「Hill of wind」 _ 15

Yellow Ginkgo Leaf _ 17
Sister in Law _ 19
Travel _ 21
Autumn Mountain _ 23
Ocean _ 25
Tiger Moth _ 27
The Geoga Bridge _ 29
At the corner of winter _ 33
Winter Ocean _ 35
Hill of wind _ 37
Cicada _ 39
Summer Field _ 41
Hometown _ 43
Birch Tree Grove _ 45
A new hometown _ 47
Rain Shower _ 49
A Trip to Guam _ 51
A Night in Vienna _ 53
Trip to Ephesus _ 55
Flashback _ 57

| 목차 |

시가 오는 봄 _ 58
정월 대보름 _ 60
일본 대지진 _ 62
봄나들이 _ 64
감동의 영화 _ 66
딱정벌레 _ 68
골동품 거리 _ 70
골목 카페에서 _ 72
들꽃 _ 74
뻐꾹 시계 _ 76
단속 카메라 _ 78
공룡 발자국 _ 80
루비네 농원 _ 82
어느 성탄의 밤 _ 84
아우슈비츠 수용소 _ 86
오월이 오면 _ 88
기차 여행 _ 90
돌멩이 하나 _ 92
양동마을 _ 94
진달래 _ 96
태종대 _ 98

| Contents |

Spring with Poetry _ 59
Full Moon in January _ 61
The Earthquake in Japan _ 63
Spring Visit _ 65
A Touching Movie _ 67
A Beetle _ 69
Street of Antiques _ 71
A Café in an Alley _ 73
Wild Flowers _ 75
Cuckoo Clock _ 77
Speed Camera _ 79
Dinosaur Footprints _ 81
Rubine Plantation _ 83
One Christmas night _ 85
Auschwitz Concentration Camp _ 87
When May Comes _ 89
A Train Trip _ 91
One Stone _ 93
Yangdong Folk Village _ 95
Azalea _ 97
Taejongdae _ 99

| 목차 |

설원 _ *100*
몽골의 아이들 _ *102*
어머니 _ *104*
백두산 오르기 _ *106*
사량도 _ *108*
종이 장미(Paper Roses) _ *110*
태틀지 국립공원 _ *112*
뭉게구름 _ *114*
오크 섬의 아침 _ *116*
선한 목자교회 _ *118*
외할미의 마음 _ *120*
그레이하운드 버스 _ *122*
여름날 _ *124*
반딧불 _ *126*
첫돌을 축하하며 _ *128*
토마스 기차 _ *130*
해무 _ *132*
눈 _ *134*
기도 _ *136*

작품해설 삶의 여행과 영원의 세계 / 최원철 _ *140*

| Contents |

Snowy Fields _ *101*
Children of Mongolia _ *103*
Mother _ *105*
Climbing Mt. Baek Du _ *107*
Saryagdo _ *109*
Paper Roses _ *111*
Tereji National park _ *113*
Fluffy Clouds _ *115*
A Morning on Oak Island _ *117*
Good Shepherd Church _ *119*
Heart of a Grandmother _ *121*
Greyhound Bus _ *123*
Summer Day _ *125*
Firefly _ *127*
First Birthday _ *129*
Thomas the Train _ *131*
Sea Fog _ *133*
Snow _ *135*
Prayers _ *137*

Explanation of the work

Life Journey and Eternity World / Won Chul Choi _ *141*

| 서시 |

바람의 언덕

바람의 언덕에 올라
저 멀리 에메랄드빛 바다에
외로운 작은 섬들을 본다

굽이굽이 돌아가는 산자락엔
온갖 고난을 겪은
소나무 숲이 해풍에 흔들리는데

내 마음은 어느덧
그물에서 고기를 털어내는
어부가 된다

욕심을 털어내고
삶의 찌꺼기조차 털어내는
선창가의 바람이 시원하다

| Prologue |

Hill of wind

*Climbing a hill of wind
I observe the small lonely islands
On the far emerald sea*

*At the foot of the mountain
With winding turns
A downtrodden old pine forest
Trembles in the ocean breeze*

*In my heart
I am a fisherman
Shaking fish from the net*

*Shaking out greed
And the residues of life
In the cool breeze on the pier*

노란 은행잎

노란 잎은
길 떠나기 싫은 몸부림으로
내 마음을 스산하게 물들이는데

포근한 융단 되어 길을 덮으면
엄마의 가슴처럼
아름답다

노란 잎이 햇빛에 비쳐지면
아스라이 멀어져간 님
노란 그리움으로 덧칠된다

오늘도 길 위에 구르는 낙엽은
나의 삶에 깊숙이 들어와
상념의 날개를 편다

Yellow Ginkgo Leaf

Yellow leaf
Colors my heart dreary
Not wanting to leave

When they cover the street like a carpet
It's pretty like a mother's bosom

The sun on the yellow leaf
Paints the lover who left like a dream
With a yellow of longing

The leaf rolling down the street
Is now part of my life
Unfolding its winged thoughts

시누이

시누이는
무엇이 그리 바쁜지
한마디도 남기지 않은 채
하늘로 훨훨 날아갔습니다.

영정 속의 모습은
오열하는 가족에게
한마디도 말도 없었습니다.

살아 있음이
가장 귀한 버팀목인 것을
이제 느끼게 됩니다

누이는 자유롭게
우리의 품을 떠나도 기억되리니
편안히 잠드소서!

Sister in Law

My sister in law
So busy leaving
Flew away to heaven
Without a word

From within her portrait
She quietly observed
Her wailing family

Now I know that
Being alive is the most precious support

Our sister left us freely
But we will remember her
Rest in peace!

여행

다른 삶이 어떤지
여행을 한다

화려함도 가난함도 느껴보며
이곳저곳 둘러봐도
하늘만은 파랗다

인생의 가는 길
이처럼 달라도
노래하는 마음은 하늘에서 왔음인지
마냥 아름답다

언젠가 기억이 흐려지더라도
긴 여행 떠나며
곳곳에서 모아온 음반을 들으련다.

Travel

I travel
To see other lives

Experiencing glamour and poverty
I look around here and there
But the sky is still blue

The journey of life can be different
A singing heart is beautiful
It must be from heaven

Some day when my memories fade
I will go on a long trip
And listen to music from other places

가을 산

그리움이 가을 산에 걸려 있는데
따스한 햇살은
상념에 젖어든다

계곡물에 비추인 모습
젊은 날은 어디론가 가버리고
가을 산만 멍하니 하늘을 본다

이끼긴 바위에 걸터앉아
옛 시절을 회상하면
그리움이 곁에 와 나를 감싼다

저물어가는 노을 속에
의지할 산이 있어 행복하다고
되뇌어보면서 잠자리에 든다.

Autumn Mountain

Longing hangs on the autumn mountain
Warm sunshine is deep
In thoughts

A shadow on the valley stream
Youth has faded away, and
The autumn mountain gazes at the sky

Sitting on a mossy rock
Reflecting on the past
Longing comes and embraces me

In the falling sunset
I lay down to sleep
Happily reminding myself
That I have a mountain to lean on

바다

출렁이는 파도는
오히려
고요한 내면의 세계를 보게 합니다.

분노의 심연엔
그리움이 있어
넘치지 않게 합니다

넓은 가슴으로
반기는 님이 있기에
평화롭게 모두가 잠들 수 있나 봅니다

보고 싶어질 때면
내 노래 수평선 넘어갈 때까지
그대 이름 불러봅니다.

Ocean

Rolling waves
Let me
See the quiet inner world

In the Abyss of wrath
There is longing
To keep it from overflowing

We can all sleep peacefully
Because of our loved ones
Who greet us with open arms

When I miss you
I call your name
Until my song flies over the horizon

부나비

당신의 창가에 새어나는 불빛으로
부나비 되어 날아든다.

정열로 태워 없어질 삶에
불붙이며 날갯짓한다

인생의 뒤안길에
파편이 되어 흩어지더라도

살아온 날들이 잊힐지언정
당신을 향한 부나비 된다.

Tiger Moth

I become a moth
Flying into the light
Peeking into your window

I flap my wings
Kindling the fire to life
That will be burned out by passion

Even if I will be shattered into pieces
In the back roads of my life

The days of my past; forgotten
I will be a moth for you

거가대교

수억 년 외롭게 지내던
섬으로 둘러둘러 길이 뚫렸건만
이젠
더욱 가까이 볼 수 있는
기적이 일어났다.

거대한 부산신항만을 지나
끝없이 이어진 어장 위로
하얀 갈매기 날갯짓에
환상의 길이 열리는데

바다 위를 걸어가던 베드로처럼
긴 다리가 덤성덤성
섬으로 걸어간다

설레임으로 가고 있는
나
쪽빛 바다 아래엔
나를 부르는 미지의 해저 터널이 있다

The Geoga Bridge

A new road to the Island
Was alone for millions of years
By connecting island to island
It is a miracle
To see it so closely

Past the gigantic New Port of Pusan
Above the endless fishery
A fantasy road opens
With the flapping of seagull wings

Just as Peter walked on the sea
A long bridge walks to the island
With big steps

I go
With a fluttering heart
Below the indigo ocean
The undersea tunnel calls me

나의 막힌 생애를 확 뚫어내듯
터널을 지나
숱한 이야기가 서려 있는
이제, 섬이 아닌 그 섬에서
노년의 멋진 삶을 그려 본다

Passing through the tunnel
As if piercing through my clogged life
In that island
Now, no longer an island
I plan a wonderful life for my old age

겨울의 길목에서

산 언덕배기
속살을 드러낸 나무들은
차가운 바람에 비명을 지르는데
둥지의 새들은 두려움에 떤다

숲 속에서는 암꿩의 울음소리
이름 모를 새들의 지저귐은
애절한 삶의 절규이런가.

건너편 마을 교회 종탑 위로
검은 까치가 까악 거리며 날아가고
하얀 눈은 검게 물들고 있다

겨울을 지나는 길목
빠알간 우체통에
설레는 편지보다 쓰레기가 차는데
사람의 마음은 점점 영혼에서 떠난다

At the corner of winter

On the hilltop
The trees expose their bare skin
Scream at the cold wind
Birds shiver in their nests with fear

The cries of hen pheasants and
Chirpings of unknown birds
Are the screams of a sorrowful life

In the village on the other side
A black magpie flies
Over a church bell tower
The white snow fades to black

The winter passes just around the corner
There is more trash than longing letters
In the red mail box
Our hearts are disappearing from our souls

겨울 바다

유난히도 추운 날
광안대교 너머 바다에는
눈부신 은빛 물결에 가슴 적신다

사랑이 운무 되어 나를 덮을 때
앞을 보지 못하던 옛 시절
수 십 년 지나도 생각이 난다

외줄을 타듯
그네를 타듯
살아온 세월

광안리 해변에 서면
겨울 바다에 찾아드는 바람만
외롭다

Winter Ocean

On a very cold day
On the Gwangan Bridge
Shiny silvery waves touch my heart

I still remember decades ago
When I could not see the future
Eyes clouded and misted over by love

Life in the past was
Like walking on a rope
Like playing on a swing

At Gwangan Li beach
The wintery beach wind
Feels lonely

바람의 언덕

바람의 언덕에 올라
저 멀리 에메랄드빛 바다에
외로운 작은 섬들을 본다

굽이굽이 돌아가는 산자락엔
온갖 고난을 겪은
소나무 숲이 해풍에 흔들리는데

내 마음은 어느덧
그물에서 고기를 털어내는
어부가 된다

욕심을 털어내고
삶의 찌꺼기조차 털어내는
선창가의 바람이 시원하다

Hill of wind

Climbing a hill of wind
I observe the small lonely islands
On the far emerald sea

At the foot of the mountain
With winding turns
A downtrodden old pine forest
Trembles in the ocean breeze

In my heart
I am a fisherman
Shaking fish from the net

Shaking out greed
And the residues of life
In the cool breeze on the pier

매미

뜨거운 여름이
막바지에 이른 아침
비 피하려 날아온 매미 한 마리

하늘이 금방 개이자
귀가 따가울 정도로
부엌 창문에서 울어 댄다

사랑을 불태우고
고난을 불태웠던 지난날
매미처럼 실컷 울고 싶다

아직도 타오르는 삶의 애착을
가슴에 간직한 채
매미 우는 소리 들으며 하늘을 본다

Cicada

One morning
At the end of a hot summer
A cicada flew in
To escape the rain

When the sky brightened
It sang in the kitchen window
Tingling my ears

Old days
With burning love
And burned troubles
I wish to cry like the cicada

With a burning attachment to life
In my heart
I lift my eyes and listen to the song

여름 들녘

먹물 구름이
소나기 내리는
들녘을 호령한다

상념의 보물창고에 가득한
그리움이
빗물이 되어 흐르는데

어느새
백일홍이 되어
붉디붉은 잎으로 피어난다

빗물이
밭고랑 사이를 지나는데
나는 자장가를 부르는 할머니가 된다

여름 들녘에 잠드는 아이들 위해
나는 삶의 부채를 들고
진종일 더위를 식힌다.

Summer Field

Dark clouds
Rule over
The showering field

Longing
Flows like rain
Filling the treasure chest of thoughts

Now
It becomes Zinnias
Blooming in red petals

The rain runs in furrows
And I become a grandmother
Singing a lullaby

For the children falling asleep
In the summer field
I cool the heat all day
With my fan of life
Hometown

고향

책가방 매고 뛰어가던 어린 시절
소들은 되새김하며 졸고
고삐 풀린 망아지는 외양간 주위를 맴도는데
하늘은 매우 푸르렀다

뭉게구름은 풀을 뜯는 소 떼를 지키는데
우르릉 꽈 앙
천둥과 번개가 번득이면
방앗간으로 줄행랑 놓던 고향이 그립다

지금은 추억 저편의 머무는 고향 풍경
엄마의 음성이 들려오던
논두렁 밭이 그리워 왠지 눈시울을 적신다

언제면 가볼까
북녘의 하늘 아래
눈물의 고향을……

Hometown

When I was young
I ran with my books on my back
The cows had dozed off while thinking
A runaway colt circled the stable
The sky was very blue

Fluffy clouds guarded herds of grazing cattle
And when the thunder crashed and the lightning flashed, we ran to the mill
I miss my hometown

Now, the scenery of hometown rests only in the corners of my memories
My eyes well up
Missing the ridges of rice paddies and fields
Where I could hear my mother calling

When will I see
My hometown of tears
Under the Northern sky

자작나무 숲

희뿌연 자작나무
북유럽에 모여
오월을 만든다

내 가슴을 휘젓던
삶의 길에 허무한 회한이
자작나무 숲 속에서 옷을 벗는다

에덴동산에서 살던 꿈
발걸음을 멈추고
여기서 꾸고 싶다

신선한 영혼을 호흡하려
자작나무 숲 속에서
머물고 싶다

Birch Tree Grove

Hazy birch trees
Gathered in northern Europe
Became May

Futile remorse for my life journey
Stirred my heart
Unveiled in the grove of birch trees

Here, I want to stop my journey
And dream
About my life in the Garden of Eden

I want to stay in the birch tree grove
To give my soul
A fresh breath

정들면 내 고향

고향이 어딘가 물어 오면은
가슴이 답답하고
머리가 헷갈린다.

황해도에 태어나 실향민 된 부모님
서울에서 태어난 나
생활은 부산에서…

타향이 고향이고
고향이 타향인 나의 운명은
가는 곳이 고향이라 말할 수 있죠

어려움과 고난을 헤치며
살아온 나날들
이렇게 정들면 고향이 아니런가.

A new hometown

If they ask me where my hometown is
My heart stops
I get confused

My parents were born in Hwang-hae-do
But they lost their hometown
I was born in Seoul
But grew up in Pusan…

My destiny makes strange towns my hometown and hometown a strange town
So wherever I am is my hometown

In a life of hardships and troubles
When it becomes endearing
It is my hometown

소나기

애타는 나의 심정
여름의 가뭄인데
갑자기 소나기가 퍼붓는다.

컨테이너 천정을 두드리는 소리는
잠시 일손을 멈추게 하는데
작은 안식처가 고마워진다

땅의 목을 축여주고
세파에 시달린 먼지조차
씻어내는 비가 부러워진다.

우울했던 마음을
소나기로 씻고
하늘을 우러러 두 손을 모은다.

Rain Shower

Rain is showering over
My anxious heart
Like a summer drought

The sound of rain on the roof
Stops my working hands
And I am grateful for my small shelter

I envy rain
That wets the thirsty soil
Washing away the weary dust of life

Washing my depressed heart
With a rain shower
I put my hands together
And look up at the sky

괌 여행

뜻밖의 여행
후끈한 열기의 괌섬

폭우가 내리더니
금방 개이는 변덕에도

검은 얼굴의 원주민은
낙천적인 삶은 낙원을 만든다

탐욕에 찌든 마음
푸른 바다에 씻어내고
이곳에 살고 싶어라

A Trip to Guam

An unexpected trip
To an island of heat

It is fickle to be so sunny
After a storm

Dark faced natives
Built a paradise
With their optimistic life

I want to wash my greed-soiled heart
In the blue ocean
And make my home here

비엔나의 밤

비엔나는 가을비에 젖는데
모차르트의 초상이 나부낀다

선술집의 늦은 밤
늙은 악사의 아리랑 연주는
눈가에 고향 하늘이 이슬로 적신다

목청 높여 합창하는 이국땅의 밤
지친 삶을 털어내고
와인에 적실 때 그리운 이가 보인다

여행자들의 노랫소리가 울려 퍼지는
비엔나의 밤거리엔
생의 기쁨이 노래와 함께 별이 된다

A Night in Vienna

In a city soaked with autumn rain
A portrait of Mozart flutters

Late night in a pub
An old artist plays Arirang
My eyes fill with dew
Thinking of the sky over my hometown

We sing out together
A night in a foreign land
Shedding our tired lives
I see my beloved in my wine glass

The sound of travelers singing resounds through the streets of Vienna at night,
The joy of life becomes a star with the song

에페소 여행

아르테미스 여신을 외치던
군중은 간데없고
구경꾼만 웅성이는데

화려했던 도시조차 사라지고
무너진 돌기둥만 나뒹구는
역사의 허무함을 본다

돌같이 굳어지고
메마른 내 마음엔
옛 사도바울의 흔적이 남아 있어

에페소의 외침이
환청으로 들려오듯
울려오는 나의 귓전

Trip to Ephesus

The crowd shouting for Artemis
Is nowhere to be found
Only the spectators are buzzing

Extravagant city has disappeared
Only the vanity of history
Is in the fallen stone pillars

In my dried and stoned heart
There is a trace of old St. Paul

The shouting of Ephesus
Rings in my ears
Like a hallucination

회상

솔향기로 젖어 있는
구덕산 고갯길

구불구불 이어진 골짜기엔
집 없는 종탑만 서 있다

신을 향한
뜨거운 마음일랑
바람에 날아가고

회색빛 요양원에
갈 곳 없는 영혼들만
힘없이 서성인다.

Flashback

The slopes of Gudeok Mountain
Filled with pine scent

At the winding stretch of the valley
Stands an uncovered bell tower

A passionate heart for God
Flew away with the wind

Only the lost souls of
Grey retreat center
Are feebly loitering

시가 오는 봄

봄은
소리 없이 오는데

치마폭에 햇살이 내릴 때면
잡풀의 새싹도 기지개 편다

동토에서 깨어나지 못한 내 마음
이제 움이 틔려나

심연에 잠자던 사연들이
펜을 따라 아지랑이처럼 피어난다

Spring with Poetry

Spring
Arrives quietly

When the sun shines on me
Sprouts of weeds stretch out too

My heart still sleeps
in the frozen ground
Waiting to sprout

All the stories of sleeping in the Abyss
Are hazed out by a pen

정월 대보름

복이 액운을 밀어내는
정월 대보름

백운포의 잿빛 하늘엔
온통
소원을 담은 흰 종이만 타오른다.

딸만 셋인 어미는
아들 하나 점지해 달라는
소원이 불길 따라 치솟는다.

까맣게 타버린 할머니 마음
누가 알랴마는
함께 밤하늘에 소원이 흩날린다

Full Moon in January

Full moon in January
Good fortune chases away bad luck

Grey sky over Dolomite beach
Full of burning white paper
Written with hopes

Hope of a mother with three daughters
Rises in a blaze
A hope for a son

Who would notice the blackened heart
Of an old woman
But, it also has hope burning to pieces
In the night sky

일본 대지진

세상이 흔들거려
종말을 예고하듯
모든 것을 휩쓸고 간 자리

혈육을 찾는 비통함이
여진餘震으로 초토화된 잔해에
뒹굴고 있다

푸른 바다는
무서운 소용돌이를 치며
고통의 눈물로 붉게 되었다

비록 슬픔을 받은 이웃이지만
고난을 이겨내라고
염원의 마음을 보태어 본다.

The Earthquake in Japan

The world shook
As if foretelling the end
A trace after everything was swept away

Cries of those
Searching for their beloved ones
Echo in the scorched remains
of the aftershock

Blue Ocean
Whirling with frightening waves
Glistens red with painful tears

To our mourning neighbors
I send my wish
For hope in their time of hardship

봄나들이

춘삼월
훈훈한 바람에
매화 꽃망울이 흔들거리는데

길가에 앉아
나물을 파는 거친 할머니의 손이
봄으로 젖어 있다

꽃 바람 따라
무리지은 나들이객들은
봄의 한가운데를 걷는다

얼음에게 발목 잡힌 섬진강은
이제 유유히 흐르는데
심란했던 마음 흘려보내고

발길 닿는 대로 걷는 길 엔
매화 꽃잎이 하나둘씩
낙화 되어 내 상념에 수를 놓는다

Spring Visit

In March
Plum blossom buds
Flutter in the warm breeze

An old woman's rough hands
Selling greens on the street
Are spirited with spring

Visitors clustered
In the flowery breeze
Walk in the center of spring

Sumjin River with one ankle in the ice
Flows slowly
I throw a worrisome heart in the stream

As my feet lead the way
One after another
Falling plum blossom petals
Embroider my thoughts

감동의 영화

"그대를 사랑합니다"
잔잔한 파문을 일으키는
영화 한 편

가난의 굴레에서
곰삭아 허물어진 몸이건만
노부부의 사랑에 적셔진 나의 눈언저리

요양원으로나 가야 할 운명인
나의 노후는
가슴 한편에 왠지 서러움이 서린다

세월에 고달픈 지아비의
고단한 어깨를 향해
영화의 제목을 되뇌어 본다.

A Touching Movie

"I love thee"
A movie that left a gentle ripple

A crumbled body buttoned up
In the yoke of poverty
The love of an old couple wet my eyes

Destined for a nursing home
In my old age
Sadness tints a corner of my heart

To the tired shoulders of the husband
Tired of life
I repeat the title of the movie

딱정벌레

긴 겨울과 함께 알에서 깨어난
딱정벌레
낡고 허름한 간이 화장실 안이
그들의 아지트이다

온통 냄새에 찌든 보금자리에서
살아가는 생명
나의 내면에도
생명이 살 수 있을까

언제 채우려나 나의 욕망을
딱정벌레도 살 수 없는
허기진 나의 뱃속

A Beetle

A beetle hatched from an egg
After the long winter
Nested in
An old and shabby portable potty

Life
In the nest
Ingrained with foul odors
Could a life live in me

When will I be able to fill my desires
Not even a beetle can live
In my hungry stomach

골동품 거리

잡동사니가 모인
골동품 거리
대신동은 복잡하다

숱한 사연을 간직한
삶의 숨결이
흔적 되어 흐른다

나의 손때 묻은 세간들
머지않아 이곳에서
손님들을 기다리지 않을까

찍찍거리며 돌아가는
낡은 전축에서
'인생은 나그네'가 봄비에 흐른다

Street of Antiques

Street of Antiques
With all the gathered junk
Daesindong is hectic

The breath of life
Treasuring many stories
Welters as evidence

My well-thumbed furnishings
May soon be waiting for customers here

From an old record player
Turning with noise
"Life is a passer" plays
In the spring rain

골목 카페에서

낯선 골목 카페에 앉아
밖을 내다보는데
전봇대 광고가 어지럽다

월세방 놓음,
알바생 구함
애환의 그림자 같다.

얼싸안고 포옹하는
젊은이들
전봇대 애환과는 대조적이다

유럽의 낯선 골목에서
흠칫 멈추었던 발걸음의 기억이
커피를 마시며 쓴웃음 짓는다.

A Café in an Alley

At a café in an unfamiliar alley
I looked out the window
At posters scattered on an electric pole

Monthly rent available,
Part time student wanted
They look like shadows of our sorrow

Embracing and hugging
Young people
Contrast the sorrows on the electric pole

The memory of a stop
In a strange alley in Europe
Gives me a bitter smile as I sip coffee

들꽃

슬로바키아 타트라 산맥
들꽃 팔아 살아가는 슬픈 할머니
눈시울 적시며 여행을 한다.

희미한 눈, 거친 손으로
관광객에 쥐여주는
들꽃송이에 어쩐지 삶의 아픔이 스민다.

함께 온 어느 부인의 남편
무주구천동 산골짜기에 사시는 노모 생각에
모두가 찡하게 울려오는데

관광버스에 실린
들꽃 같은 우리의 애달픈 인생
끝도 없는 미지의 산길을 달려가고 있다

Wild Flowers

A sad old woman
From the Tatra Mountains in Slovakia
Makes a living selling wildflowers
And travels with wet eyes

The pain of life emanates
From her blurry eyes and rough hands
As she sells wildflowers to travelers

Someone with us
Is reminded of his elderly mother
In a valley of Moo-joo-gu-chun-dong
Our hearts feel a sharp pain

Our sorrowful lives are
Like wildflowers on a tourist bus
On an endless unknown mountain road

뻐꾹 시계

정적을 깨고
뻐꾹 뻐꾹
시계 소리에 집안은 온통 활기에 찬다.

오스트리아에서 낯선 이국으로 시집 온
뻐꾹새는
외로운 노부부의 집에서도

고향 하늘 그리운지
하루 종일
시간마다 울어 댄다

고향이 그리워
슬퍼하는 뻐꾹새
오늘도 뻐꾹, 내일도 뻐꾹

Cuckoo Clock

Breaking the silence
Cuckoo Cuckoo
The sound fills the house with energy

A Cuckoo clock from Austria
Ended up at a lonely old couple's house

It must miss its home sky
It cries every hour
All day long

The sad Cuckoo clock
Missing home
It cuckoos today
And tomorrow

단속 카메라

올빼미의 붉은 눈알이
나를 무섭게 쏘아본다

휴대폰에 삐리리~ 뜨는 문자
'신호 위반'

과태료 생각에 돋는 소름
기분이 엉망이다

단속 카메라가 부끄러워
얼굴 못 들 날이 언제 오려나

Speed Camera

A red owl's eye
Glares at me awfully

I receive a text message
"Traffic violation"

The thought of a fine gives me goose bumps ruining my mood

When will the time come
That I cannot hold up my face
Shameful of the speed camera

공룡 발자국

썰물에 드러난
억 만년 전에 살았던 공룡발자국

으르렁거리는 소리는 파도가 되어
한 맺힌 울음을 울고 있다.

공룡보다 못한 나의 족적
어디에 남길까

차라리 상족암 공룡발자국에
내 마음만 담으련다

Dinosaur Footprints

A dinosaur from countless ages past
Left footprints revealed after a low tide

Their roars have become waves
Crying their sorrowful cry

Where will I leave my legacy
Though smaller than the dinosaur's

I'd rather fill the dinosaur footprints in Sangjokam with my heart

루비네 농원

예안리 산비탈에
마음을 심는데
수년이 걸렸다

땅을 갈고 허리 휘고
풀 뽑다가 손 베이는
고통의 순간들

배꽃처럼 하얀 꽃
닮으려는 내 마음
벌써 꽃은 떨어지려 하는데

뿌린 만큼 거두는 기쁨으로
헛된 욕심 버리고
오늘도 땀 흘리며 땅을 일군다

Rubine Plantation

It took years
To plant hearts
On the mountain slope of Yeah-Ri

Painful hours
Plowing the soil with bent backs
Cutting the fingers on the weeds

My heart yearns to be
Like the white pear blossoms
With petals ready to fall

For the pleasure of harvesting
As much as we sow
We plow the ground with sweat today
Throwing away the vain greed

어느 성탄의 밤

깊어가는 성탄의 밤에
환희에 빛나는 별 하나
온 누리를 햇빛보다 밝게 비추는데
어쩐지 내 마음엔 어둠이 깃든다

머잖아 외로운 십자가
나도 질 수 있을까
근심으로 채워진 내 마음에
도마가 찾아온다.

어두움이 뒤덮는 세상에
회칠한 무덤 속에 두어야 할 이기심
뚫고 나오는 데
참회의 눈물로 씻어본다

십자가를 향한
통곡의 눈물은
맑아지는 내 영혼에 덧입는
환희의 노래가 된다

One Christmas night

In the deep night of Christmas
A star shines with jubilance
Brighter than the sun
But the darkness sinks in my heart

Could I carry
that lonely cross?
Thomas comes to my heart
Filled with worries

The world covered with darkness
Selfishness, buried in a grave and painted with plaster, still pokes out
I try to wash it with penitent tears

The tears of lament
Coating my clearing soul
Become a jubilant song

아우슈비츠 수용소

음산한 수용소
보는 이로 하여금 경악케 한다.
나는 할 말을 잃었다

알몸은 간데없고
수많은 해골들과 유품들엔
죽음의 가스만 스며 있다

할퀸 역사의 상처
숨죽이면서 보는 나
박애의 정신이 무언지 혼란에 파묻힌다

오랜 시간 지났건만
철조망 사이로 플라타너스가 줄지어 서
그때의 슬픔을 잎들만 반짝이며 울고 있다

Auschwitz Concentration Camp

Gloomy concentration camp
Astonishing to look at
I was rendered speechless

Naked bodies were nowhere to be found
Only the gas of death was infused
in so many skeletons and articles

Holding my breath
I looked at
The scars of ravaged history
What is the spirit of Philanthropy?
I am in confusion

A long time has passed
There stands a line of Sycamore trees
Shiny Sycamore leaves shake with grief through the barbed wire fence

오월이 오면

오월이 오면
붉은 장미 꽃잎에
불타오르는 내 사랑

그대의 심장에
진한 향기를
황홀함으로 남기고 싶다

지금,
그대 소식 알길 없어
세월만 애태우며 흐르고 있다

또다시 오월이 오면
이제는
그대 사랑을 놓치지 않으련다.

When May Comes

When May comes
My love blazes up
On the red rose petals

I want to leave a strong scent
Like ecstasy
In your heart

Now,
Time is passing in agony
Not knowing where you are

If May comes again
Then
I will not lose your love

기차 여행

기차는
끝없는 레일 위로
나를 싣고 달리고 있다

해변의 부서지는 파도가
나의 여정을
꿈속으로 끌어들인다

파란 눈의 할머니 친절한 모습에
내가 과연 저럴 수 있을까
혼자만의 여행을 뒤돌아보게 한다

인생의 철로 위에
무거운 짐 가득 싣고
달려온 여정

언젠가 내려놓을 짐들을 보며
오늘 하루 여정을
되돌아본다.

A Train Trip

A train
Running on an endless rail
Is carrying me

The breaking waves on the beach
Entice my journey
Into a dream

The kindness of a blue-eyed old lady
Makes me reflect on my trip alone
Can I be like her?

A journey on the rail of life
I ran
Carrying a heavy load

Looking at the baggage
I will unload someday
I reflect on
Today's journey

돌멩이 하나

돌탑 위
삶의 애환의 돌멩이 하나 올려놓고
염원을 하건만

돌 같이 굳어만 가는
나의 마음

세월과 함께 쌓아가는
바벨탑

발버둥치는 혼탁한 세상
구원할 신神께 빌어본다

One Stone

On a stone tower
I pray to add
The stones of life's joys and sorrows

My heart hardens
Like a stone

I will build the Tower of Babel
With time

I pray to the Savior
For the struggling corrupt world

양동마을

구름 따라 밀려든
많은 여행객
옛 선비 발자국 따라서 간다

선비의 기백이 서린
고가古家 마당엔
쓰레기가 수북하다

하루에 참을 인忍
백번 쓴다는
서백당書百堂

참지 못하고
남의 맘에 상처를 준
세 치 혀가 부끄러워진다

Yangdong Folk Village

Travelers surge in
With the clouds
Tracing the footsteps of old scholars

In the yard of the old house
In tribute to the spirit of scholarship
Are mounds of trash

In Seobaekdang
They wrote "Patience"
One hundred times a day

I feel ashamed of my tongue
Saying words that hurt others
Without patience

진달래

산자락 허리에
연분홍 진달래로 두른 치마가
꽃바람에 살랑인다.

꽃잎에 입 맞추는
나를 보고
심술궂은 바람은 꽃잎을 흔드는데

보다 못한
벗나무의 하이얀 꽃잎이
내 머리 위로 살포시 앉는다.

서산마루에
떠나가기 싫은 님처럼
황령산 봉우리에 물든 분홍빛

Azalea

The skirt of light pink Azaleas
Wraps the mid slope of the mountain
Blossoms flowing in the breeze

A wicked wind flutters the flower petals
As I bend to kiss them

A white cherry blossom petal
Gently lands on my head

A lover standing mid-mountain
Not wanting to leave
Gazes at the pink-tinted peak of Hweng Ryeong Mountain

태종대

숲길 사이
쏟아지는 햇살에
연초록 새순이 빤짝거리고

겨우내 움츠렸던 육신에
숲 속은
새 생명을 불어넣는다

서로 마주 보며
밀어를 나누는 나무들 사이로
넓은 바다는 말이 없는데

해변에 쪼잘 대는 모래알은
바닷속 이야기를 들려주는 파도에게
그리운 이의 안부를 물어본다

행복한 소식을 싣고 오는 봄바람에
지그시 눈을 감고
아름다운 봄내음에 취하여 본다

Taejongdae

Between the alleys of a forest
Are new sprouts of light green
Shining in the pouring sunlight

The forest breathes
And new life enters
My winter-shrunken body

The trees face each other
Sharing secret words
Through them I see the vast quiet ocean

The chattering sand on the beach
Asks about missing loved ones and
The waves tell stories from the seafloor

The spring breeze brings happy news
And I close my eyes
Intoxicated by the scents of spring

설원

순백의 설원에
멈추어 버린 시간도
하얗게 변했다

보고 싶은 순록은 보이지 않고
지붕마다 맺혀 있는
고드름이 순록의 뿔과 같다

쏟아지는 햇살은
내 마음을 녹이는데
한 방울 한 방울 떨어지는 고향 생각

서서히 다가오는 떠나야 할 날
돌아갈 곳 있음에
뿌듯한 가슴

근심 걱정 모든 것
눈 속에 묻어 두고
설원을 빠져나와 꽃피는 나라로 돌아가련다.

Snowy Fields

In the white snowy fields
Time stands still and fades to white

I wanted to see reindeer
but none are in sight
The icicles remind me of their antlers

Pouring sunshine melts my heart
Out drips thoughts of hometown
One by One

Departure is approaching soon
Having a place to go back to
Makes my heart full

Worries and troubles buried in the snow
I will escape the snowy fields and return to the blooming land

몽골의 아이들

우리와 비슷한 풍속이 많은 곳
무언가 기대되는
울란바트로

웬일일까? 길가엔 떠도는 고아들
빈민촌에 필요한 눈물과 기도
잃어버린 꿈을 찾아주려 필요한 손길

까만 어린 눈동자 속에
그래도 내일이 있는 듯
빤짝이며 빛을 내는 몽골 어린이

지금은 내 가슴이 미어지고 슬퍼도
배움터 위하여 한층 한층 벽돌을 쌓으며
저들을 위하여 기도하는 내 마음

Children of Mongolia

With many similar customs
I have expectations for
Ulaanbaatar

What happened to the orphans in the street?
Send prayers and tears for the Ghetto
Help them find their lost dreams

Tomorrow still exists
In the young black eyes
The Mongolian child is still twinkling

My heart is breaking and saddened now
I lay bricks for their school one by one
My heart weeps for them

어머니

1·4 후퇴 때 피난 내려와
넉넉지 않은 살림살이
늘상 베풀며 사셨던 믿음의 어머니

방내리 촌집에
호박이랑 고추랑 심으셨건만
노후에 자식들의 효도도 못 받고

병마로 인해
무더위가 기승부리던 어느 해
눈물 없는 곳으로 가신 어머니

수십 년이 지났건만
어머니가 체취가 그리워져
방내리로 달려가 보면

마당가 깊은 우물엔
어머니 모습 닮은
주름진 내 얼굴만 비추인다

Mother

Fled during the January-Fourth Retreat
With her insufficient life
My faithful mother always shared

In the country house in Bangnae-ri
She planted squash and peppers
Unable to enjoy her children's devotion

Losing the battle with illness
In a year with extreme heat
She went to the place of no tears

After many decades
I run to Bangnae-ri
When I miss the scent of my mother

I find my wrinkled face
Looking like my mother
In the deep well in the yard

백두산 오르기

민족의 혼이 있는
백두산에
유월이 왔다

채 녹지 않은 눈 사이
비바람 모진 고통을 이기고
소록이 피어나 조그만 민들레

가까이 다가간 천지호에는
정지된 듯 고요한 심연에
탄성이 퍼진다

장백산 흐르는 온천물에
삶은 계란으로 요기를 면하고
따끈한 커피의 향기에 몸을 추스르며

기쁨의 눈물로
두 손 들어 만물의 조물주인
하나님을 찬미한다

Climbing Mt. Baek Du

June has come to Mt. Baek Du
Vessel of the Spirit of our people

Between patches of snow
Small dandelions bloom quietly
Enduring the pain of wind and rain

Approaching Lake Cheon Ji
Exclamations spread out
To the quietly paused abyss

In the hot springs of Mt. Changbaek
Satisfying hunger with a boiled egg
Bodies warmed by scents of hot coffee

With joyful tears and arms raised
I praise God
The creator of the world

사량도

곱고 맑은 물길에 목욕한 다도해가
환상처럼 떠오르는 바다에
끝없이 펼쳐지는 수평선에 마음이 설렌다

무속신앙 판치는 이곳이라 듣고서
연말에 선한 일 하겠다고
건너갔건만

벌써 누군가 여기에
모진 고난과 핍박을 견디고
나약한 몸으로 세운 십자가

뱀과 같은 모양으로 이루어진 섬
하나님의 복음이 이루어짐에
절로 머리가 숙여진다

Saryagdo

Bathing in pretty and clear water on an archipelago island
The endless horizon, rising up like a fantasy
Makes my heart flutter

I heard it is full of Shamanism
So I crossed the ocean at the end of the year
Wanting to do some good

A feeble body already erected a cross
Having endured suffering and persecution

On an island shaped like a snake
I bow down my head
To the accomplishment of God's good news

종이 장미(Paper Roses)

종이인지 자연 장미인지 모를 장미꽃
구별도 못하는 우리의 눈
어떻게 누군가를 사랑할 수 있을까

후회에도 소용없는
떠나간 사랑에
눈물로 당신을 그리워한다

세월이 흘러도
당신이 다시 온다면
기어코 놓치지 않을 내 마음

뜨겁고 변치 않는
가슴으로
맞이할 당신

Paper Roses

Unable to tell
If the roses were real
Or made of paper
How could I love someone

Regret is useless compensation
For lost love
And tears of longing

Even now,
If you would return to me
My heart would not let you go

I would embrace you
With a passionate and
Everlasting heart

태를지 국립공원

끝이 보이질 않는 황량한 대평원
한 폭의 그림 위에 놓여 있는
태를지 국립공원 가는 길

길 위에 무리지어 쉬는 들소들
말몰이하는 유목민들의 삶이
왠지 부럽다

척박한 대지 위에 피어나는 야생화
끈질긴 생명은
몽골인의 순박한 미소며

사막의 오아시스 같은 태를지
게르 천막의 하룻밤은
지친 심신에 감동의 파고가 높아만 간다

Tereji National park

Desolate plains with no horizon in sight
The road to Tereji National Park
Runs in a picture

A herd of buffalo resting on the road
Makes me envy the life of a nomad herding horses

Wild flowers blossoming on barren soil
The na?ve smiles of the Mongols
Reflect their perseverance

Tereji is like an oasis in a desert
A night in a tent in Ger
Moved my tired body and soul

뭉게구름

놀츠 캐롤라이나의
금빛으로 반짝이는 모래가
끝없이 뻗쳐 있는 사우스 비치

하늘 가득 채운 뭉게구름 속에
두고 온 고국의 그리운 얼굴들
모래톱에 휩쓸려 사라지는데

밀려오는 파도에
외로움만 떠다닌다.

낯설고 물설은
광활한 하늘에
그리운 소식 담아 띄우고 싶어라

Fluffy Clouds

The endless sand shines gold
At South Beach
North Carolina

In the sky full of fluffy clouds
Longing faces left in my homeland
Disappear with the sandy bank

Only loneliness
Floats on the surging waves

I want to fly a letter of homesickness
In the vast sky
Of strange faces and strange waters

오크 섬의 아침

오크 섬의 바다에서 갓 나온 태양은
아침을 깨우는데
고요한 마당에
풀잎 사이 찌르레기 소리가 조심스럽다

축복이 이슬처럼 내리는
이 섬에는
천진난만한 사람들이 모여 사는데
떼 지어 노니는 검은 부리 갈매기조차
여유롭다

아름다운 생명들이 숨 쉬는 해변에
포말을 그리며 부딪치는 파도는
아쉽게 떠나는 내 마음을 아는지
왔다가 밀려가고 또 밀려가며
아침을 바다로 밀어내고 있다

A Morning on Oak Island

Sun rises over the ocean
Awakening the dawn
A starling chirps in the grass
In a quiet garden

On this island
With blessings like dew
Innocent people live together
Even the flocking seagulls are peaceful

On the beach full of beautiful lives
Breaking waves make parabolas
Sensing my sad departing heart
They push mourning into the ocean
Waving in waving out

선한 목자교회

숲 속의 전원에
선한 목자의 미소가 어린다

오월의 푸르름 위에 놓인
십자가 둘레에 조잘거리는 카딜라

모든 것이 찬양하는 소리와 모습
떠나온 가슴에 살아나는 광경

가난하지만 베풀 수 있는
작지만 큰 교회

먼 이국땅에 뿌리내려
믿음으로 살아가는 우리의 성도

이 땅에서 복되고 천국에서 복되리
빛의 직분 다하는 선한 목자교회

Good Shepherd Church

The smile of the Good Shepherd
Spreads over the forest

Cadila chatters around the cross
Sitting in the green of May

Everything resounds with praises
That will remain in my heart

They are poor but they share
They are small but big

Rooted in a foreign soil
They are faithful disciples

Be blessed on earth and be blessed in heaven
The Good Shepherd Church is fulfilling its duty as the light of the world

외할미의 마음

아들인들 어떻고
딸인들 어떠하랴
아들을 바라는 부모의 마음

인간사 멋대로 되지 않는데
스트레스 속에 사는 착한 딸래미

두근거리는 가슴으로 낳은 아이인데
네 번째도 딸,

가슴이 와르르 무너져 내리는
외할미의 심정을 누가 알랴

새 생명 주신 것도 너무나 감사해
십자가를 의지하며 눈물 닦는다.

Heart of a Grandmother

They say it doesn't matter
Whether it's a girl or a boy
But the parents wish for a son

Human life doesn't go as planned
My kind daughter lives a stressful life

She gave birth with an anticipating heart
But it was her fourth daughter

Who could know
The crushed heart of a grandmother

I am thankful for a new life
Leaning on the cross, I wipe my tears

그레이하운드 버스

두렵고 설레는 마음으로
월밍턴행 버스를 타고
얼굴색 다른 낯선 사람들과 함께 여행한다.

젖무덤을 드러낸 중년의 흑인 여자
징징거리며 보채는 아이
보기가 안쓰럽다

아들이 멀리 떠나는 듯
포옹하며 손 흔드는 백인 노부부
나그네 삶이 여기에 있다

고달픈 삶을 실은 버스는
폭염이 지글거리는 아스팔트 위를 외로움을 토하며
달리고 있다.

Greyhound Bus

With a fearful and fluttering heart
I board a bus to Wilmington
Traveling with strangers

A middle-aged black woman with her breast showing
I was sorry to see the whining child

An old white couple hugs and waves
Son must be leaving far
The lives of travelers

A bus carrying tired lives
Runs on asphalt burning with heat
Vomiting its loneliness

여름날

폭염이 이어지는 긴 여름날
몸뚱이는 더위에 흐느적거리고
머릿속은 텅 비어져 간다.

거리조차 열기에 숨이 막히고
한낮은 고요 속에 잠들지만
나의 손가락은 노트북 위에 춤을 춘다

허기진 욕망을
실타래 풀듯 풀어내려고
시詩만 바쁘게 마음 안팎을 넘나든다.

Summer Day

A long hot summer day
My body sways in the heat
Emptying my head

Streets suffocate in the heat
Noon falls asleep in silence
My fingers dance on the keyboard

To unravel my hungry desires
Like a skein of thread
Poetry beats into and out of my heart

반딧불

어둠이 내려앉은 여름밤 하늘
반딧불이 황홀하게 포물을 그린다.

빌딩 숲과 오염에 가려 못 보던
반딧불은
내 영혼에 불을 붙인다.

어릴 적 밤하늘에 별을 세던
옛 동무는
어디서 무얼 하며 사는지

한여름 밤의 꿈으로 다가온
반딧불 춤사위에
추억 속의 여름밤은 황홀하다

Firefly

In the summer night sky
Settled with darkness
A firefly draws a blissful parabola

Hidden in a forest
Of buildings and pollution
The firefly lights a fire in my soul

What could my old friend be doing and where
We used to count the stars in the night sky when we were young

With the dance of the firefly
Like a summer night dream
The summer night in memory is blissful

첫돌을 축하하며

주님이 주신 생명
세상에 첫 울음을 터트린 날
우린 감격의 눈물을 흘렸지

선한 눈망울로 방긋방긋 웃을 땐
우린 행복해서
찬양의 노래를 불렀지

아파서 칭얼거리고 울 때엔
우린 너무 가슴이 아파서
주님께 기도드렸지

첫 돌을 맞이해서
귀한 생명을 주신 주님께
감사 예배를 드려야지

시냇가에 심은 나무처럼
사랑받는 아이로
잘 자라다오, 신혁아!

First Birthday

A life given by God
The day we heard your first cry
We all shed tears of joy

When you smiled with kind eyes
You made us sing praises
With happiness

When you whined in pain
Our hearts broke
And we prayed to the Lord

On your first birthday
Let us worship the Lord
who gave us precious life
With thanksgiving

Sinhyuk!
Grow up to be a healthy
and lovable child
Like a tree planted by the stream

토마스 기차

손자 아이가 애띤 미소로
다가와 뽀뽀를 한다

토마스 기차만 보면
사달라고 떼쓰기 바쁘고

혼자서 장난감을 동생 삼아
하루 종일 소곤소곤 이야기한다.

그 녀석이 가고 나면
허전해하는 할아버지

거실 한 편에 흘리고 간
토마스 기차 하나가 우두커니 서 있는데

우리가 지나고 난 자리에
무엇을 세상에 남을 것인지……

Thomas the Train

Grandson kisses grandpa
With a child's smile

Whenever he sees Thomas the Train
He asks Grandpa to buy it for him

He talks to his toy softly all day
As if it were his little brother

Grandpa feels empty
After he is gone

In the corner, sitting quietly
Lies a piece of Thomas the train

What will we leave behind
After we pass from this world⋯.

해무

해변에는 해무에 잠겨
앞이 보이지 않고
도심 속엔 안개비가 스민다

그리움도
외로움도
추억 속에 묻고

먼 앞을 보려고 애써보지만
장님과 같은 신세
현실의 수렁 속에서 허우적거린다.

저 멀리 영도의 등대의 빛줄기
나에게 비춰오는데
해무를 뚫고 노 저어 갈 수 있을까?!

Sea Fog

I can't see anything
On the beach buried in the sea fog
In the city, it is raining

I bury longing
And loneliness
In my memories

I try to see far ahead
But I am blind
I struggle in the pit of reality

Young-do lighthouse
Shines its light on me
Could I row across through the sea fog?!

눈

찬바람에 흩날리는 눈은
나뭇가지 휘돌아 감기고
댓돌 밑에 내려앉는다.

문지방 열고 밖을 보면
세상은 황홀경으로 빠져들고
내 마음조차 하얗다.

지난 세월과 잊었던 사연은
미끄럼 타듯 구르고
후회와 아쉬움만 남는다.

지금은 어디메 있는지 알 수 없지만
기다려 보는 마음만 차가웁게 떨고 있는데
바람 소리만 윙윙거리며 지나가고 있다

Snow

Blown in the cold wind
It swirls around a tree branch
And lands under the terrace stones

Looking out over the threshold
The world falls into ecstasy
My heart is flooded with white, too

The memories forgotten with time
Roll down like a slide
Only the regrets and sorrows remain

I don't know where it is now
My longing heart trembles in the cold
I only hear the sound of the passing wind

기도

기도가
나와 함께 있으니
외롭지 않고

당신이
나와 함께 있으니
두렵지 않고

당신의 사랑에
삶의 아름다움이
내 마음에 넘치네.

기도로
빛이 보이고
삶이 능력을 얻는다

기도로
저 천국을 바라보는데
내 마음은 기쁨으로 충만타.

Prayers

I am not lonely
Because
Your prayers are with me

I am not fearful
Because
You are with me

Because of your love
The beauty of life
Overflows in my heart

With prayers
I see light and
My life is strengthened

With prayers
I see heaven
And my heart is full of joy

| 작품 해설 |

삶의 여행과 영원의 세계

최 원 철

| Explanation of the work |

Life Journey and Eternity World

Won Chul Choi

| 작품 해설 |

삶의 여행과 영원의 세계

- 김혜영의 작품 『바람의 언덕』에 대하여 -

최 원 철

(부산대학교 명예교수, 시인, 수필가)

　김혜영 시인의 첫 작품인 『바람의 언덕』은 시어詩語들이 모두 쉬워 난해難解한 곳이 거의 없다. 작품에 나타나는 시詩에 대한 해설을 할 필요조차 없다고 본다. 시詩는 어려워야 하는 것이 결코 아니기 때문이다. 김 시인의 시는 독자들이 그대로 읽고 나름대로 이해하면 된다. 그러나 여기에서 시詩 속에 나타나는 김 시인의 삶의 세계를 설명해 보고자 한다.

　릴케[Rainer Maria Rilke]는 시詩가 체험體驗이라고 하였다. 육순六旬을 맞이하는 김 시인은 서울에서 출생하여 서울로 피난 온 부모님과 함께 부산에서 정착하게 되었다. 실로 많은 고난과 역경을 이겨내고 지금처럼 아름다운 삶을 영위하기까지는 긴 인생 여정을 노래하기는 충

| Explanation of the work |

Life Journey and Eternity World

- Regarding Hyeyoung Kim's 『Hill of Wind』 -

Won Chul Choi

(An Emeritus Professor at Pusan National University, Poet, Essayist)

For her first work 『Hill of Wind』, Hyeyoung Kim used a relatively simple structure, which makes it easy to understand. There is no explanation required for this poem, which is good, because poetry should not be difficult to understand. The reader should be able understand Kim's poetry with almost no effort. However, I would like to explain Ms. Kim's life world, which is reflected in her poems.

Rainer Maria Rilke once said that poems are experiences. Poet Kim, who will soon turn 60 years old, was born in Seoul, and fled to other cities with her parents before settling down in Busan. Actually, she was forced to undergo many troubles and hardships before she was able to enjoy the beautiful life that she currently lives, and it is those experiences that enable her to sing

분한 체험을 하였다고 말할 수 있다.

> 바람의 언덕에 올라
> 저 멀리 에메랄드빛 바다에
> 외로운 작은 섬들을 본다
>
> 굽이굽이 돌아가는 산자락엔
> 온갖 고난을 겪은
> 소나무 숲이 해풍에 흔들리는데
>
> 내 마음은 어느덧
> 그물에서 고기를 털어내는
> 어부가 된다
>
> 욕심을 털어내고
> 삶의 찌꺼기조차 털어내는
> 선창가의 바람이 시원하다

- 「바람의 언덕」 전문

이글에서 '바람의 언덕'과 같은 세파世波의 절정의 산봉우리에 올라 뒤돌아보면 아름다운 세상에서 작은 섬들과 같은 작은 피안의 섬들도 있음을 발견하게 된다. 비록 그곳에서라도 굽이굽이 돌아가는 삶의 길이 놓여 있고 비바람에 찢겨지기도 하고 흔들리기도 하지만 그 섬에서 피안을 느끼며 그물에서 걷어 올린 고기를 털어

of such a long life journey.

> Climbing a hill of wind
> I observe the small lonely islands
> On the far emerald sea
>
> At the foot of the mountain
> With winding turns
> A downtrodden old pine forest
> Trembles in the ocean breeze
>
> In my heart
> I am a fisherman
> Shaking fish from the net
>
> Shaking out greed
> And the residues of life
> In the cool breeze on the pier

- Full text from 「Hill of Wind」

In this poem, the author has climbed to the top of a mountain, the 'Hill of Wind' which represents the climax of a life of hardship, and has looked back to find that her life journey had encompassed little hill-islands in a beautiful world. Although there is curved life path that must be followed and it has been torn and swayed by rain and storms, the author becomes a fisherman shaking fish from the net while experiencing nirvana

내는 하나의 어부가 된다. 이것은 자연의 현상과 김 시인의 시적 감각이 함께 어우러짐을 알 수 있다. 인간도 자연의 한 분자와 같이 자연을 이루고 있는 구성원이기에 자연과 더불어 그 자연 속에서 진리를 찾는 것이 당연할지도 모른다. 그뿐만 아니라 김혜영 시인은 그녀가 가지는 모든 욕심을 삶의 그물에서 털어내는 선창가의 어부가 되는 것이다. 이는 마음속 깊이 잠재하고 있는 시적 감각이나 시적 재능을 표출하여 예술로 승화시키는 역량을 가지고 있다고 생각한다.

김 시인은 인생을 살아가는 것이 여행객이 여행하는 것과 다를 바 없음을 깨닫고 이 평범한 사실 속에서 진솔한 시를 돌출해 내고 있다. 아래의 『여행』에서 얻어지는 아름다움을 음미하고 있음을 볼 수 있다.

> 화려함도 가난함도 느껴보며
> 이곳저곳 둘러봐도
> 하늘만은 파랗다
>
> 인생의 가는 길
> 이처럼 달라도
> 노래하는 마음은 하늘에서 왔음인지
> 마냥 아름답다
>
> — 『여행』 부분

on that island. This reveals the harmony between the nature phenomenon and Ms. Kim's poetry sense. Since humanity is one of the elemental parts of nature, like a molecule, perhaps that's why humans seek harmony with nature to find the truth within nature. In addition, Poet Hyeyoung Kim becomes a fisherman on a quay; where she shakes her greed from the net of life. I believe that the author is capable of sublimating her potential poetry sensation or poetry ability, and honing it into an art.

She realizes that life is a journey, and so she infuses her poems with the simple truth. We can see that she has tasted the beauty that is acquired from 「Travel」 which is the title of the next poem.

> Experiencing glamour and poverty
> I look here and there
> But the sky is still blue
>
> The journey of life can be different
> A singing heart is beautiful
> It must be from heaven
>
> - Partial text from 「Travel」

여행이라는 것은 휴식도 포함되겠지만, 새로운 세계의 끊임없는 탐구다. 여행을 하며 이곳저곳 둘러보면 온갖 화려함도 가난함도 느끼게 된다. 이것은 여행에서 오는 방관자의 입장에서 보는 것이기에 형편은 달라도 파란 하늘은 공통적으로 같다. 그렇지만 이 여행자는 인생의 가는 길이 많이 달라도 즉 여러 가지 자기들의 환경이 달라도 시적으로 노래하는 그 마음은 하늘에서 내려준 특권이기에 마냥 시인의 마음은 즐겁고 아름답다.

이와 같이 김 시인은 현실의 바쁜 생활을 잠시 뒤로하고 많은 여행으로 세계를 두루 다니며 색다른 곳마다 거기에서 얻어지는 이미지를 통하여 사물과 감성에 대한 인식을 새롭게 느끼고 있는 것이다.

> 탐욕에 찌든 마음
> 푸른 바다에 씻어내고
> 이곳에 살고 싶어라
>
> - 『괌 여행』 부분

여기에서는 한적하고 아름다운 태평양 남쪽의 괌에서는 일상생활을 잠시 뒤로 미룬 체 바쁜 생활에 얽매인 탐욕으로 찌든 마음을 푸른 바다에 씻어내며 괌에서 살고 싶음을 솔직히 고백하고 있다.

Although traveling includes leisure time, it is still a constant exploration of the new world. While looking around here and there as we travel, we can experience all kinds of luxuries and poverty. Since this view is from a bystander from traveling, the situation may be different, but they have the blue sky in common. However, the poet feels happy and her mind is beautiful since the singing poetic heart was granted to her from heaven, in spite of their different life paths and their different environments.

Likewise, she set her busy life aside and traveled the world, where she gained new recognition and realizations about life and sensations through the images that she acquired.

> I want to wash my greed-soiled heart
> In the blue ocean
> And make my home here

- Partial text from 「A Trip to Guam」

Through this poem, at a quiet and beautiful south pacific island, Guam, she confesses her desire to live in Guam by washing her greed-stained mind in the blue ocean and putting her routine life aside for a while.

김혜영 시인은 여기에 만족하지 않는다.

> 선술집의 늦은 밤
> 늙은 악사의 아리랑 연주는
> 눈가에 고향 하늘이 이슬로 적신다
>
> 〈중략〉
>
> 여행자들의 노랫소리가 울려 퍼지는
> 비엔나의 밤거리엔
> 생의 기쁨이 노래와 함께 별이 된다

— 『비엔나의 밤』 부분

위의 시詩에서 여행의 기쁨 속에서 늘 마음을 떠나지 않는 것은 고향 하늘이 그리워 옴을 읽을 수 있다.

『에페소 여행』, 『아우슈비츠 수용소』, 『기차 여행』, 『몽골의 아이들』, 『백두산 오르기』, 『뭉게구름』, 『오크 섬의 아침』, 『그레이하운드 버스』 등에서 어디론가 가고 싶은 열망에 따라 가 보고 우리가 한 번도 경험하지 못했던 새로운 시공간을 체험하고 우리의 삶을 노래하며 여행을 한 것을 느끼게 한다.

그리고 김 시인의 일반적인 삶의 바탕은 어떠한가?

She is still not satisfied with it :

　　Late night in a pub
　　An old artist plays Arirang
　　My eyes fill with dew
　　Thinking of the sky over my hometown

　　<Ellipsis>

　　The sound of travelers singing resounds through the streets of Vienna at night,
　　The joy of life becomes a star with the song

　　　　　　　　　　- Partial text from 「A Night in Vienna」

From the above poem, we can see that while having fun from traveling, the author still misses the sky over her hometown.

In the poems 「A Trip to Ephesus」, 「Auschwitz Concentration Camp」, 「A Train Trip」, 「Children of Mongolia」, 「Climbing Mt. Baekdu」, 「Cumulus」, 「A Morning on Oak Island」, and 「Grey Hound Bus」, the author endulges her desire to go somewhere by traveling and she experiences new spaces and time, and sings about life to share the things she learned on her journey.

Then, what is the foundation of her routine life?

노란 잎은
길 떠나기 싫은 몸부림으로
내 마음을 스산하게 물들이는데

〈중략〉

오늘도 길 위에 구르는 낙엽은
나의 삶에 깊숙이 들어와
상념의 날개를 편다

- 『노란 은행잎』 부분

위의 시詩에서 우선 김혜영 시인은 육순의 문턱에 들어서려는 찰나에 서서 인생의 참뜻을 살펴보는 시간을 갖는다. 즉 젊을 때의 철부지 한 노란 사랑은 이미 지나, 몸은 비록 세월을 비켜가지 못하기에 길 위에 구르는 낙엽을 볼 때에 깊은 상념에 빠지는 것을 그대로 들어내고 있다. 아무리 훌륭한 인간이라도 허무하게 사라질 낙엽과 같지 않을 수 없는 것이다. 세월이 지나 같이 동고동락하던 시누이마저 이별한 김 시인은 더더욱 삶의 허무함을 느끼고 있지만 『시누이』에서 신神의 세계로 그 정신이 전이轉移 되는 것을 알 수 있다.

시누이는
무엇이 그리 바쁜지

Yellow leaf
Colors my heart dreary
Not wanting to leave

<Ellipsis>

The leaf rolling down the street
Is now part of my life
Unfolding its winged thoughts

- Partial text from 「Yellow Gingko Leaf」

From the above poem, the author takes time to review the true meaning of life before stepping through the door to her 60s. Beyond the immature yellow love of youth, the author expresses that she has fallen deep in thought when she sees the fallen leaves rolling in the street, and realizes that our bodies cannot escape from the ravages of time. No matter how great one is, one will ultimately disappear like a fallen leaf, in vain. In 『Sister In Law』, the author's sister-in-law has passed away, causing the author to realize the vanity of life, but I feel that the poem also reveals that the author's thoughts have ascended and that she is able to perceive the world from God's point-of-view.

My sister in law
So busy leaving

한마디도 남기지 않은 채
하늘로 훨훨 날아갔습니다.

영정 속의 모습은
오열하는 가족에게
한마디도 말도 없었습니다.

〈생략〉

- 『시누이』 부분

 이 세상에서 더 살아야 하는 시누이가 돌연 한마디 말도 남기지 않고 하늘나라로 훨훨 떠나버렸다고 한 것을 볼 때 영혼의 존재를 믿는 것을 알 수 있다.
 살아가면서 만남도 중요하지만, 이별도 대단히 중요하다. 돌연히 이별해야 함도 있고, 망설이다가 이별하기도 하고, 못내 서럽거나 함께하기는 힘들어서 하는 경우가 있다. 여기에서는 이별하지 않아야 할, 느닷없이 닥친 이별을 아쉬워하는 것이다. 이 이별에는 기다림도 사라져 버려야 할 그런 이별인 것이다. 김 시인은 시누이와 사이가 상당히 좋았던 모양이다. 아쉬움을 '하늘로 훨훨 날아갔습니다.' 라고 허탈함을 나타내는 동시에 남아 있는 가족들의 오열 속에서도 영정 속의 시누이는 '한마디도 말도 없었습니다' 라는 시어로 더욱더 간절함을 강조하였다.

Flew away to heaven
Without a word

From within her portrait
She quietly observed
Her wailing family

<Ellipsis>

- Partial text from 「Sister in Law」

In this poem, it is evident that the sister-in-law, who is still needed by her loved ones, has suddenly fled this life without a word, and it seems that the author believes in the existence of an afterlife.

In our life, the people we meet are very important, but leaving is also very important. Sometimes, we have to leave suddenly, are hesitant to leave, or leave because of the hardships or sorrows from being together. In this poem, the author is saddened by the sudden and unexpected separation that allowed no waiting. Maybe the author had a very good relationship with her sister-in-law. She expresses her dejected feelings in the phrase 'Fled to the sky' and also emphasizes her desperate feelings when she observes that the departed left 'Without a word' to her family, who weeps aloud.

바다 위를 걸어가던 베드로처럼
긴 다리가 덤성덤성
섬으로 걸어간다

설레임으로 가고 있는
나
쪽빛 바다 아래엔
나를 부르는 미지의 해저 터널이 있다

나의 막힌 생애를 확 뚫어내듯
터널을 지나
숱한 이야기가 서려 있는
이제, 섬이 아닌 그 섬에서
노년의 멋진 삶을 그려 본다

- 『거가대교』 부분

  거가대교를 잇는 섬들을 갈릴리 호수를 건너는 성서에 나오는 베드로를 비교했다. 예수가 물 위로 걸어오라는 명령으로 제자 베드로는 믿음 하나로 걸어가다가 물 위로 어떻게 걸어가는가라는 의심이 들자마자 다리가 물속으로 빠지게 된 일화가 있다. 그래서 베드로가 걸어가는 발자국을 섬으로 보고 '바다 위를 걸어가던 베드로처럼/긴 다리가 덤성덤성/섬으로 걸어간다' 라는 거가대교를 의인화시켜서 섬으로 이어 있음을 표현하였다.
  그리고 처음으로 개통된 거가대교를 '설레임으로 가

Just as Peter walked on the sea
A long bridge walks to the island
With big steps

I go
With a fluttering heart
Below the indigo ocean
The undersea tunnel calls me

Passing through the tunnel
As if piercing through my clogged life
In that island
Now, no longer an island
I plan a wonderful life for my old age

- Partial text from 「The Geoga Bridge」

  The Geoga Bridge is compared to St. Peter who walked on the Sea of Galilee in the bible. When Jesus told him to walk on the water, St. Peter showed his faith in Jesus by obeying, but when he doubted, he sank into the water. So the author adds anthropomorphic character to the Geoga Bridge, comparing the islands it connects to St. Peter's footsteps, and to express this, she says 'Just as Peter walked on the sea/A long bridge walks to the islands/With big steps'.

  Also to express that Geoga Bridge is completed and opened

고 있는/나/쪽빛 바다 아래엔/나를 부르는 미지의 해저 터널이 있다' 여기에서 또다시 다가오는 미지의 세계인 터널과 그 뒤에 오는 섬이 어떤 것일지에 대한 암시를 망각할 수 없는 점으로 설정되어 있다. 시는 가급적 감정을 절제하여 예술로 승화시켜야 좋은 시라고 말할 수 있지만, 김혜영 시인의 시는 대체적으로 감정을 절제하기보다 아이러니컬하게도 오히려 가지고 있는 관념과 정서를 잘 융합해서 나가는 것이 특징이다. 전통적으로 감정을 절제해야 한다는 논리가 맞겠지만, 그 속에서 끝없는 우리의 정서를 환기시키며 이끌어 냄도 그리 나쁘지는 않다고 생각된다.

여태껏 살아오는 과정에서 시 속의 화자의 '막힌 생애를 확 뚫어내듯/터널을 지나/숱한 이야기가 서려 있는/이제, 섬이 아닌 그 섬에서/노년의 멋진 삶을 그려 본다' 그 짜임새가 물 흐르듯 흐르고 있다.

> 기차는
> 끝없는 레일 위로
> 나를 싣고 달리고 있다
>
> 해변의 부서지는 파도가
> 나의 여정을
> 꿈속으로 끌어들인다

to the public, she says 'I go/With a fluttering heart/Below the indigo ocean/The undersea tunnel calls me'. It implies the unknown world 'tunnel' and the islands that come behind as something unforgettable. In good poems, emotions are restricted as much as possible to sublimate the art; however, her poems ironically combine conceptions and emotions very well instead of restricting them. The logical restriction of emotions would be correct in tradition; however, I think that it is also good draw our emotions out by refreshing them continuously.

When she says 'Passing through the tunnel/As if piercing through my clogged life/In that island/Now, no longer an island/I plan a wonderful life for my old age' she alludes to the fact that the structure of her life flows like water.

As if removing the barriers from life/I dream of coolness in my old age/Through the tunnel/At that island which is no longer an island/There are many stories.

>   A train
>   Running on an endless rail
>   Is carrying me
>
>   The breaking waves on the beach
>   Entice my journey
>   Into a dream

파란 눈의 할머니 친절한 모습에
내가 과연 저럴 수 있을까
혼자만의 여행을 뒤돌아보게 한다

인생의 철로 위에
무거운 짐 가득 싣고
달려온 여정

언젠가 내려놓을 짐들을 보며
오늘 하루 여정을
되돌아본다.

- 『기차 여행』 전문

  위 시詩에서 삶의 기차를 타고 가는 김혜영 시인은 아름다운 해변의 파도처럼 온갖 삶의 계획들이 생겼다가 부서지는 꿈과 같은 여정에 외국인들의 친절한 모습에 나도 저렇게 행복 해 질 수 있을까 생각하면서 혼자 여행을 하게 된다. 그렇지만 무거운 세상 짐을 잔뜩 지고 가는 이 여정이 끝날 때를 생각해 보며 여태껏 걸어온 길을 뒤돌아보기도 하는 상념에 잠기기도 한다.
  김 시인은 유럽 여행을 하면서 자연환경이 아름다움을 느끼고 있는 듯하다. 그래서 언젠가 다다를 영원히 머물고 싶은 곳을 생각하게 된다. 아마도 스웨덴이나 노르웨이 같은 곳에 수많은 자작나무 숲을 보면서 느꼈을 게다.

The kindness of a blue-eyed old lady
Makes me reflect on my trip alone
Can I be like her?

A journey on the rail of life
I ran
Carrying a heavy load

Looking at the baggage
I will unload someday
I reflect on
Today's journey

- Full text from 「A Train Trip」

    The author travels alone on the train life. Just as life plans are made, and then break down like waves on a beach, she sees a foreigner being so kind, and wonders if she can be that happy. However, she thinks about the end of this journey, burdened by the heavy luggage of life, and fall into deep thoughts while looking back at the path she has traveled.

    It seems that she is also enjoying the beautiful natural environment while traveling Europe, and thinking about where to finally retire. Maybe she saw the many birch forests that can be found in Sweden or Norway.

희뿌연 자작나무
　　　북유럽에 모여
　　　오월을 만든다

　　　내 가슴을 휘젓던
　　　삶의 길에 허무한 회한이
　　　자작나무 숲 속에서 옷을 벗는다

　　　에덴동산에서 살던 꿈
　　　발걸음을 멈추고
　　　여기서 꾸고 싶다

　　　신선한 영혼을 호흡하려
　　　자작나무 숲 속에서
　　　머물고 싶다

　　　　　　　　　　　　- 『자작나무 숲』

　북유럽의 오월의 자작나무라는 자연에 대한 요소와 허무한 회한이라는 관념의 합일을 이루어 자연과 인간의 뗄 수 없는, 즉 하나의 구성요소로서 그 의미가 나타남을 알 수 있다. 옛날 인간의 최초 낙원이었다는 에덴동산에서 부끄러움과 괴로움 없이 살던 그곳을 연상하며 머물기를 원하고 있다.
　그래서 아름다운 자작나무 숲 속에서 살고 싶은 마음을 말한다. 그러므로 이 자작나무 숲이 자아내는 의미를

Hazy birch trees
Gathered in northern Europe
Became May

Futile remorse for my life journey
Stirred my heart
Unveiled in the grove of birch trees

Here, I want to stop my journey
And dream
About my life in the Garden of Eden

I want to stay in the birch tree grove
To give my soul
A fresh breath

- Full text from 「Birch Tree Grove」

   A natural element 'the birches in May in Northern Europe' is combined with the conception of vain regret, implying that nature and humanity cannot be separated. She associates this with the Garden of Eden, humanity's first paradise where there was no shame or agony, and she reveals her yearning for the Garden in her desire to live in the beautiful birch forest. The meaning of the birch forest is combined with the life in the Garden of Eden to create the image of the author

에덴동산의 생활과 합일시켜 나가면서 그 속에 시인이 존재하게 되는 이미지를 낳게 한다.

> 깊어가는 성탄의 밤에
> 환희에 빛나는 별 하나
> 온 누리를 햇빛보다 밝게 비추는데
> 어쩐지 내 마음엔 어둠이 깃든다.
>
> 머잖아 외로운 십자가
> 나도 질 수 있을까
> 근심으로 채워진 내 마음에
> 도마가 찾아온다.
>
> 어두움이 뒤덮는 세상에
> 회칠한 무덤 속에 두어야 할 이기심
> 뚫고 나오는 데
> 참회의 눈물로 씻어본다
>
> 십자가를 향한
> 통곡의 눈물은
> 맑아지는 내 영혼에 덧입는
> 환희의 노래가 된다.
>
> － 『어느 성탄의 밤』 전문

이 시詩를 통하여 우리는 김혜영 시인의 종교관에 대한 박식함을 느끼게 된다. 즉 기독교인으로서의 신앙의 경지境地가 상당히 깊다고 보겠다. 성탄일이 되면 예수의

who exists within.

> In the deep night of Christmas
> A star shines with jubilance
> Brighter than the sun
> But the darkness sinks in my heart
>
> Could I carry
> that lonely cross?
> Thomas comes to my heart
> Filled with worries
>
> The world covered with darkness
> Selfishness, buried in a grave and painted with plaster, still pokes out
> I try to wash it with penitent tears
>
> The tears of lament
> Coating my clearing soul
> Become a jubilant song

- Full text of 「One Christmas Night」

Through this poem, we are given insight into the author's religious beliefs. It is evident that she is a deeply faithful Christian. At Christmas, people decorate christmas trees to

성탄을 기념하기 위하여 아름다운 크리스마스트리를 만드는가 하면 갈릴리 지방의 나사렛 동네의 어느 말구유에서 태어났을 때 하늘의 큰 별이 그 위에 머물렀다는 것을 나타낸 것을 설명하기 위해 1연에 '깊어가는 성탄의 밤에/환희에 빛나는 별 하나/온 누리를 햇빛보다 밝게 비추는 데/어쩐지 –내 마음엔 어둠이 깃든다' 라는 솔직한 고백을 하였다. 모두가 기뻐하지만 내 마음속에 가지고 있는 어두운 생각, 여기에서는 언급이 없지만, 틀림없이 크거나 작거나 간에 죄에 대한 회개가 없는 그런 마음으로 성탄절을 맞이하려니 마음이 무거워 옴을 표현하고 있지 않을까 생각된다.

2연에서는 '머잖아 외로운 십자가/나도 질 수 있을까/근심으로 채워진 내 마음에/도마가 찾아온다.' 예수는 세상 사람을 구원하기 위하여 십자가에 달려 죽었는데 과연 나도 남을 위해 그렇게 할 수 있을까 하는 근심으로 채워진 마음에다 도마가 찾아온다는 것은 도마라는 사람은 예수의 부활을 못 믿다가 직접 예수의 창에 찔린 옆구리와 손에 박은 못 자국을 보고 믿게 되었을 때 예수는 직접 보고 만지지 않고 믿는 믿음이 더 큰 것을 이야기했다. 그러므로 교인으로서의 김혜영 시인의 진솔한 마음을 그대로 나타내고 있다.

3연에서는 '어두움이 뒤덮는 세상에/회칠한 무덤 속에 두어야 할 이기심/뚫고 나오는 데/참회의 눈물로 씻

celebrate the birth of Jesus, and she honestly says 'In the deep night of Christmas/ A star shines with jubilance/ Brighter than the sun/ But the darkness sinks in my heart' to explain that a big star was above Jesus when he was born in a manger in Bethlehem.

Although everyone is happy, there are dark thoughts in her mind, although unmentioned in the text, perhaps because they are receiving Christmas without repentance or contemplation of the reason for the season, and it seems to make her feel heavy.

In the second verse, 'Could I carry/that lonely cross/Thomas comes to my heart/Filled with worries', the author wonders if she could sacrifice herself as Jesus did. In the phrase 'Thomas comes to my heart', she speaks of Doubting Thomas, who didn't believe that Jesus had been resurrected until he touched the wounds in Jesus' hands and side. At that time, Jesus talked about the importance of having faith without seeing. So this poem reflects the author's honest mind as a Christian.

Verse 3 'The world covered with darkness/ Selfishness, buried in a grave and painted with plaster, still pokes out/ I try to wash

어본다.' 거쳐야 할 거추장스러운 삶에서 항상 밝은 것만 있는 것이 아니고 어둠이 엄습해 오는 이 세상에서라도 이기심이라는 것만큼은 밖으로 나오지 못하도록 하는 표현을 회칠한 무덤 속에 두어야 한다고 시인은 말하고 있으나 항상 자기에 이기심이 자꾸 튀어나오는 것을 참회의 눈물을 흘리는 아름다운 마음을 엿볼 수 있다.

4연에서 '십자가를 향한/통곡의 눈물은/맑아지는 내 영혼에 덧입는/환희의 노래가 된다.' 그리하여 기독교에 귀의한 김 시인은 앙상하고 메마른 것 같은 삶을 십자가를 향한 통회痛悔의 눈물을 실컷 흘리고 나니 나무 끝에 나오는 새순처럼 환희의 새순을 틔우고 있음을 노래하고 있다. 그래서 성탄의 밤을 절망 속에서 기쁨을 키워가고 있음을 알 수 있다. 이것이야말로 기독인들이 갖춰야 할 근본적인 마음이다. 천한 것에서 위대함으로, 가난에서 부함으로, 이끄는 절묘하고도 귀한 진리를 터득할 때 인생이 걸어가는 질서에 순응하고 신과의 합일로 지향할 때 예수로 통한 인간 구원의 세계 즉 영적인 세계에 근접할 수 있다고 보겠다.

> 책가방 매고 뛰어가던 어린 시절
> 소들은 되새김하며 졸고
> 고삐 풀린 망아지는 외양간 주위를 맴도는데
> 하늘은 매우 푸르렀다

it with penitent tears' implies that there are not always bright things in this burdensome life and that selfishness needs to be buried in a sealed tomb so that it can't come out; however, the author shows her beautiful mind when she says 'I try to wash it with penitent tears'.

In verse 4 'The tears of lament/Coating my clearing soul/Become a jubilant song', the author sings that after crying towards the cross for repentance about her dried and angular life, joy blooms like a flower bud. It shows that she had growing joy from despair on a Christmas night.

This is actually the fundamental attitude that Christians need to have. When realizing the excellent and precious truth that leads from vulgarity to greatness, and poverty to richness by complying with the order of life and orienting on Oneness with God, we can approach salvation through Jesus, which is the spiritual world.

> When I was young
> I ran with my books on my back
> The cows had dozed off while thinking
> A runaway colt circled the stable
> The sky was very blue

뭉게구름은 풀을 뜯는 소 떼를 지키는데
우르릉 꽈 앙
천둥과 번개가 번득이면
방앗간으로 줄행랑 놓던 고향이 그립다

지금은 추억 저편의 머무는 고향 풍경
엄마의 음성이 들려오던
논두렁 밭이 그리워 왠지 눈시울을 적신다

언제면 가볼까
북녘의 하늘 아래
눈물의 고향을……

- 「고향」 전문

 그래도 김 시인은 영적인 세계를 조용히 관조하면서도 자기가 자라나던 고향을 생각한다. 고향이 없는 사람은 외로운 사람이다. '책가방 매고 뛰어가던 어린 시절'과 되새김하면 졸고 있는 소와 망아지를 대조시킴으로써 평온한 농촌의 목가적인 풍경을 그려내고 있다. 그런데 여기에 푸른 하늘을 연계시킴으로 그때의 꿈은 참으로 깨끗하고 순수한 희망에 찬 것임을 연상케 한다.

 그렇지만 항상 좋을 수만 있는 것이 아니었다. '뭉게구름은 풀을 뜯는 소 떼를 지키는데/우르릉 꽈 앙/천둥

   Fluffy clouds guarded herds of grazing cattle
   And when the thunder crashed and the lightning flashed, we ran to the mill
   I miss my hometown

   Now, the scenery of hometown rests only in the corners of my memories
   My eyes well up
   Missing the ridges of rice paddies and fields
   Where I could hear my mother calling

   When will I see
   My hometown of tears
   Under the Northern sky

- Full text from 「Hometown」

While quietly contemplating the spiritual world, the author recalls her hometown where she grew up. A person who doesn't have a hometown is a lonely person. By comparing 'my childhood when running with backpack on' with 'cows and fouls who are ruminating and dozing,' she describes a peaceful pastoral farm atmosphere. Also by associating the blue sky, the author implies that her childhood dream was a very clean, pure and hopeful thing.

However, there were not always good things. 'Fluffy clouds

과 번개가 번득이면 /방앗간으로 줄행랑 놓던 고향이 그립다' 라고 했다. 아무리 좋은 고향이라도 천둥과 번개가 번득이었던 무서운 고향이라도 김 시인은 자기의 고향이 그리운 것이다. 그렇지만 지금은 가 볼래야 가 볼 수 없는 북녘땅의 고향이 되어 버려 살아생전 언젠가 가 볼 수 있을까 눈물짓는 그 고향이 지금은 실낙원이 되어버린 고향이다.

>기도가
>나와 함께 있으니
>외롭지 않고
>
>당신이
>나와 함께 있으니
>두렵지 않고
>
>당신의 사랑에
>삶의 아름다움이
>내 마음에 넘치네.
>
>기도로
>빛이 보이고
>삶이 능력을 얻는다
>
>기도로
>저 천국을 바라보는데

guarded herds of grazing cattle/And when the thunder crashed and the lightning flashed, we ran to the mill/I miss my hometown. Whether it was a good hometown or a very scary

place of thunder and lightning, the author always misses her hometown. However, her hometown is in the North, where she can not access it, and has become a lost paradise that she hopes to visit once more when she is alive.

>
> I am not lonely
> Because
> Your prayers are with me
>
> I am not fearful
> Because
> You are with me
>
> Because of your love
> The beauty of life
> Overflows in my heart
>
> With prayers
> I see light and
> My life is strengthened
>
> With prayers
> I see heaven

내 마음은 기쁨으로 충만타.

- 『기도』 전문

비록 소망이 이루어지지 않는 한이 있더라도, 기도하는 것이야말로 신자이든지 불신자들이든지 간에 현실의 염원念願을 영혼의 세계로 이끄는 진지한 순간이며 결실結實의 순간이 되는 것이다.

김혜영 시인은 남과 자신을 위해 기도하는 생활이 외롭지 않다고 했다. 기도는 반드시 대상이 있기 마련이다. 당신이라고 부르는 대상이 곧 절대자인 신神이다. 기도할 수 있는 마음뿐만 아니라, 진정한 대상이 있기에 꼭 이루어지리라는 당당한 신앙심이 있기에 두렵지 않다. 그리고 그 사랑을 느끼고 있다. 그래서 김 시인이 바라는 기도의 제목에 해결할 수 있는 빛이 보이고 시인의 삶의 능력을 갖춘다고 했다. 그다음 마지막으로 갈 수 있는 천국이라는 것 즉 영적인 세계의 고향이 있기에 기쁨이 늘 충만하다고 했다.

시를 쓴다는 것은 쉬운 일이 아니다. 시를 쓰는 데는 시의 구조를 알아야 하고 그 속에 들어 있는 내재율과 운율 할 것 없이 되도록 많은 것을 알아야 함은 주지의 사실이다. 그러나 이러한 것은 시인 자신이 만들었다기

And my heart is full of joy

- Full text from 「Prayers」

Although hope cannot be realized, praying is a serious moment of leading, whether it is a believer or non-believer, the hope of reality to the spiritual world and become the moment of realization.

The author said that a life spent praying for herself and others is not lonely, because we always have to pray for someone. The person we call You is the absolute existence, God. In addition to the mind of praying, because there is a true target and faith in prayer, and she is not afraid. She actually feels the love. As the author says from the title, there is a light for a solution and her life can be revitalized. Next, she says that because there is the hometown in heaven, and eternal life, her life is filled with joy.

It is not easy to write poetry. In order to write a poem, it is necessary to know the structure of poetry and to have high knowledge about it, including rhythm and prosody. However, it is more correct to say that it is actually made by critics rather than the author itself. Everyone has a poetic turn of mind. From children to adults, and from low classes to high classes, everyone has access to the sensibility that is available to all humans.

보다 오히려 평론가의 손에서 이루어진 것이라고 보는 것이 더 옳을 것이다. 사람은 누구나 다 시심詩心을 가지고 있다. 어린아이부터 어른에 이르기까지, 저 낮은 계층에서 높은 계층에 이르기까지 인간이라면 느끼게 되는 감성은 다 가지고 있다. 이것을 좀 더 절제와 함축성 있는 것을 절묘하게 잘 갖추어 나가야 함은 누구나 다 알고 있는 사실이다. 무던히 노력하고 자기와의 싸움을 하면서 완숙하게 되는 것이다. 그렇다고 오늘날 빈번히 시를 쓴 작가 자신조차 그 의미와 하고자 하는 말이 무엇인지조차 모르는 것을 잘 쓴 시라고 오해할 수도 있다. 시는 쉬워야 한다. 여기에서 김혜영 시인의 시는 매우 쉽다. 읽기에 좋고, 난해한 것이 없다. 그렇지만 더욱더 나타내고자 하는 것을 좀 더 압축하여 내적인 표현의 함축성을 표출하여야 할 것이다. 말하고 싶은 것을 다 표현하는 것보다, 절제하며 그 의미에 심오한 뜻을 내포하고 있음이 바람직하다. 아무리 훌륭한 시인이라도 그 작가의 시가 다 훌륭한 시가 되는 것은 결코 아니다. 김혜영 시인이 등단 후 첫 번째 내놓는 시로써 값있는 삶의 새 출발이라고 말하고 싶고, 이로 인하여 더욱더 좋은 감화력과 호소력이 넘치는 시가 되고, 또한 훌륭한 시인이 되기를 바란다.

Everyone understands that there are exquisite restrictions and implications to complete a poem. This innate knowledge can be matured through continuos efforts and internal struggling. Sometimes, it can be frequently misunderstood that even the person who wrote the poem doesn't fully understand it. Poems need to be understandable. In this aspect, Hyeyoung Kim's poems are excellent. They are easy to read and understand. However, her poems also be more compressed in order to be expressed as implications for internal meanings. It is more desirable to contain deep meaning with more restricted expressions instead of saying everything out loud. No matter how excellent a poet is, not all of their poems can be excellent. These are the first works in her literary career, and I think she is off to a good start. I believe that she will one day be an excellent poet with more appeal and influence.

김혜영 시집

바람의 언덕

2011년 11월 7일 인쇄
2011년 11월 11일 발행
지은이 | 김혜영
펴낸이 | 최장락
펴낸곳 | 도서출판 두손컴
　　　　부산광역시 부산진구 부전2동 526-12 삼성B/D 301호
　　　　전화 : (051)805-8002　팩스 : (051)805-8045
　　　　이메일 : doosoncomm@hanmail.net
출판등록 제329-1997-13호

ⓒ 김혜영 2011 대한민국
값 10,000원
* 저자와 협의에 의해 인지를 생략합니다.

A Collection of Hae Young Kim's Poems
Hill of Wind

Printed on November 7, 2011
Published on November 11, 2011
Author | Kim, Hae Young
Publisher | Choi, Jang Rak
Publishing Co. | Doosoncomm Publishing Co.
　　　　　　301 Samsung Bldg, #526-12, Bujeon2-dong,
　　　　　　Busanjin-gu, Busan, Korea (Postal Code : 614-850)
Telephone : 82-51)805-8002　Facsimile : 82-51)805-8045
E-mail : doosoncomm@hanmail.net
Registration No. : 329-1997-13

ⓒ Kim, Hae Young Korea 2011
Price : ₩10,000
* Damaged books are to be exchanged.

ISBN 978-89-97083-14-5-03810